STEVE JOBS WANTED PERFECTION

CELEBRITY BIOGRAPHY BOOKS
CHILDREN'S BIOGRAPHY BOOKS

BABY PROFESSOR
EDUCATION KIDS

In this book, we're going to talk about the amazing life of entrepreneur Steve Jobs. So, let's get right to it!

STEVE JOBS

WHO WAS STEVE JOBS?

Steve Jobs was a visionary, an inventor, and an industrial designer. He was also one of the most famous entrepreneurs of all time and a tireless perfectionist. He drove himself and his employees with his desire for the highest quality in both substance and style. Even though he was difficult to work for, many people admired his way of doing business and have tried to follow in his footsteps.

His companies, Apple Computer, NeXT Computer, and Pixar revolutionized the industries of computers, graphic design, publishing, music, animation, and communication. The Macintosh computer for graphics and desktop publishing, the iPod hand-held music device and iTunes for songs, the iPad tablet for entertainment, and the iPhone for communication were some of his most legendary inventions. The iPod, iPad, and iPhone have all made the list of the "most important inventions of the 21st century."

Steve Jobs

STEVE'S EARLY LIFE

Born on February 24, 1955, Steve was given up for adoption without a name by his biological parents. A political science professor from Syria, his biological father was named Abdulfattah Jandali. His mother Joanne Schieble worked as a speech therapist.

They were unmarried when they had Steve, but later married and had another child called Mona Simpson. Steve didn't uncover any information about his biological family until he was in his late twenties. His biological sister eventually became one of his best friends.

Mountain View, California

Steve had been born in San Francisco and his adoptive parents lived in Mountain View, California. His adoptive father Paul had been in the Coast Guard and was a machinist by trade. His adoptive mother Clara worked in accounting. Eventually the area where they were living would be known as part of Silicon Valley.

Paul loved working with his son as they dabbled with electronics in the family's garage.

Steve developed a lot of confidence and persistence working with his Dad as they took apart electronics pieces and put them back together again.

2066
House of Paul and Clara Jobs

Steve was highly intelligent, but he was bored in elementary school so he became a class clown. The only way his fourth-grade teacher could get him to focus on his studies was by offering him bribes. Later in his schooling, he took a series of tests and did so well that the school's administrators wanted him to move on to high-school early. However, his parents decided that he should continue in regular classes.

While in high school, Jobs met his future business partner Steve Wozniak, who was a student at the University of California in Berkeley. The two bonded immediately over their common love of computer chips, which are semiconductor materials that have integrated circuits. At that point in time, very few people knew the power of computer chips.

University of California

Apple 1 Computer

Wozniak had already designed and put together many computers by the time he met Jobs, but Jobs was a quick study and the two quickly delved into their passion of working with electronics for computing.

They were both very independent minded and that similarity helped them to work well together. At that time, computers were huge devices. Jobs and Wozniak had a vision of a computer that the everyday person could use on his or her desktop.

sięgowość, faktury, CRM

Desktop Computer

Reed College

THE BEGINNINGS OF APPLE COMPUTER

After Jobs graduated from high school, he attended Reed College located in Portland, Oregon, but after six months he was bored and dropped out. During this aimless period, which lasted about 18 months, he explored different creative classes including one in calligraphy that forever influenced his design sense.

Atari hired him to be a designer for their popular video games in 1974, but Steve didn't stay with them long. Instead, he went on a spiritual quest for enlightenment in India and took drugs to expand his mind. In those days, he would have been called a "hippie."

TIME BANDIT
Bill Dunlevy   Harry Lafnear
(VERSION 2.0)
BANDIT 1'S   BANDIT 2'S CONTROLLER:
CONTROLLER: (FOR THE PLAYER GAME)
JOYSTICK 2   JOYSTICK 1
PRESS F1 & F2 TO CHANGE CONTROLLERS
PRESS "1" OR "2" TO START THE ADVENTURE
Atari   SC1224
520 Station
ATARI 520ST
Atari

>AJDSHQTREGJHSBUUAQLWWABYR
I DON'T KNOW THAT WORD
>MY NAMEIS COLPANTS
I DON'T KNOW THAT WORD.
>FGDHUDAURULHWFA
I DON'T KNOW THAT WORD.
>CHRISQ
I DON'T KNOW THAT WORD.
>

apple II

Apple II

He got into vegetarianism after reading the book Diet for a Small Planet. He often went on strange diets where he would eat just carrots or just apples for long periods of time. Legend has it that he had just come back from working on an apple farm before he proposed the name "Apple Computers" for the company that he and Wozniak would start.

obs wanted the name of their company to be friendly
because their computer was meant to be personal.
Their computer would be a desktop extension of what
a person could do with some extra computing help.

He also thought it would be good if the name came before "Atari" in the phone book.

Another apple connection was the story of Isaac Newton and how he had discovered gravity after being hit in the head by an apple.

Two years after he had quit working at Atari, in 1976, Jobs and Wozniak founded Apple Computer. Their beginnings were humble. Jobs sold his Volkswagen bus and Wozniak sold his scientific calculator to cobble together the funds so that they could get started. They started their work in the Jobs Family garage.

EV-9031
IN USE
disk II
Apple II
Apple II computer
198

In a few short years, the two Steves revolutionized the computer industry. They succeeded in building computers that people found friendly and easy to use. With their combined skills, technical know-how, and the innovative marketing strategies implemented by Jobs, their company quickly became successful. Within four years, during which they launched the Apple I and Apple II, they became a public company in 1980. By the end of their first day of trading, the company was worth $1.2 billion dollars.

JOBS IS PUSHED OUT OF HIS OWN COMPANY

In 1983, Jobs hired John Sculley formerly of Pepsi-Cola to become CEO of Apple. Jobs was only 28 years old and he was still growing into his role as a visionary and leader. The next Apple products that were launched didn't do well in the marketplace.

4 YR SALES RECORD
of Seven Products
apple ///
monitor ///
THE OPEN APPLE PODCAST
Apple III

IBM computer

Computer giant International Business Machines (IBM) had become the dominant force in the personal computer market. Personal computers, called PCs for short, from IBM and other companies were running operating systems called MS-DOS built by Bill Gate's company Microsoft. Apple's computers ran off completely different operating systems and they weren't compatible. Sculley believed that the decisions Jobs was making were hurting the company.

In the meantime, Jobs was working with the design and engineering team on the Macintosh computer. The Macintosh had an easy-to-use graphical user interface (GUI), which simply means that the user double clicked a design icon to launch a piece of software.

File Edit Search Format Font Style
Untitled
Macintosh

Macintosh Plus

The Macintosh was youthful, fun, and creative. It gave designers a way to do beautiful typography and desktop publishing. It was selling well, but it didn't gain as large of a market share as MS-DOS systems.

The board of directors sided with Sculley and Jobs was pushed out of his own company in 1985.

NEW HORIZONS

After Jobs left Apple he began a new computer company called NeXT, Inc. The following year, he purchased Pixar Animation Studios, which had been owned by Star Wars creator George Lucas. Jobs believed so much in Pixar's potential that he put in a $50 million dollar investment.

NeXT Computer

PIXAR
STUDIOS
Pixar

Pixar went on to produce amazingly successful 3-d animated films such as Toy Story and Finding Nemo. In 2006, when the Walt Disney Company bought Pixar, Jobs had more shares of Disney stock than anyone else. He made more money with Pixar than he had when he was first at Apple.

COMING BACK TO APPLE

In 1997, Apple bought NeXT Computers and Steve Jobs returned as Apple's visionary CEO. His former company was really struggling. At one point, Jobs sought an investment and received it from his rival Bill Gates. With Jobs back at the top, Apple began to innovate once again.

MINITEL AND TELETEXT: LONG-RUNNING SUCCESSES
NeXT computer, NeXT Inc., US, 1990
The expensive but cutting-edge NeXT computer, whose OS evolved into Mac OS X, was famous for rapid prototyping features. These let Tim Berners-Lee create the Web in just three months, but restricted the first browser-editor to these rare machines.

MENU
iPod

They started rolling out new products like the colorful desktop iMacs and laptops. Next, they created the compact iPod, which was designed to fit a thousand songs in your pocket. Then, Apple launched iTunes software so that individual songs could be downloaded to the iPod. These products were huge hits in the marketplace.

The innovation continued with the iPhone in 2007. This new smart phone completely changed the way people were using their phones. In 2007 Apple Computer dropped the "Computer" from their name since the company was now offering so many different types of electronic devices. Their success with the iPhone was followed by another innovative product in 2010, the iPad tablet.

iPad tablet

ILLNESS AND DEATH

In 2003, doctors discovered that Jobs had a rare type of pancreatic tumor. Jobs altered his diet and looked at alternative treatments instead of going in for surgery. Many people believe that decision cost him his life.

Finally, a year later he went in for surgery, which was successful. However, he continued to become progressively sick and in 2009 he had a liver transplant. He continued to work at Apple until August of 2011 and he passed away in October of 2011. He was only 56 years old.

His legacy lives on. In 2013, Apple Computer sold 350,000 of their iPhones in one day.

Like
Social Media
Chat

Now you know more about the life and achievements of Steve Jobs. You can find more Biography books from Baby Professor by searching the website of your favorite book retailer.

Visit

BABY PROFESSOR
EDUCATION KIDS

www.BabyProfessorBooks.com
to download Free Baby Professor eBooks
and view our catalog of new and exciting
Children's Books